Practice and Pass

English Test

FLYERS

Pupil's Book

Cheryl Pelteret
and Viv Lambert

DELTA Publishing
Quince Cottage
Hoe Lane
Peaslake
Surrey GU5 9SW
United Kingdom
www.deltapublishing.co.uk

First published 2011

Project managed by Chris Hartley
Edited by Barbara MacKay
Designed by Peter Bushell
Illustrations by Geo Parkin, Alek Sotirovski and Ian West
Printed in Malta by Melita Press

ISBN: 978-1-905085-42-2

Contents

Listening PART 1

Step 1 – Prepare

1 Listen and write the words.  1

    1 an ....umbrella....

    2 a ....

    3 a ....

    4 a ....

    5 a ....

    6 a pair of ....

    7 a pair of ....

2 Find the words in exercise 1.

t	i	g	h	t	s	p	s
a	r	b	a	s	c	o	h
r	s	e	m	a	k	c	o
i	g	l	o	v	e	s	r
n	a	t	r	n	g	e	t
g	p	o	c	k	e	t	s
u	m	b	r	e	l	l	a
s	h	r	t	s	e	t	s

3 Read and write the words from exercise 2.

1 It's gold. ....ring....

2 It's silver. ....

3 It's red. ....

4 They're blue. ....

5 They've got spots. ....

6 They're striped. ....

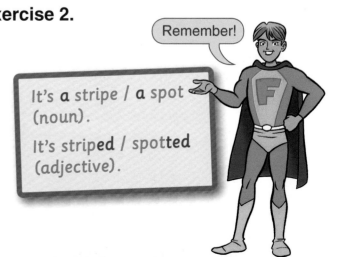

Remember!

It's **a** stripe / **a** spot (noun).

It's strip**ed** / spott**ed** (adjective).

4 Look and write the words.

1 *footballer*   2 ....   3 ....

4 ....   5 ....   6 ....

5 Look and write the words.

gold   ~~shorts~~   spot   spotted   umbrella   uniform

1 The footballer is kicking the ball. He's wearing striped ..... *shorts* ..... .

2 The fireman is driving a fire engine. He's wearing a ....

3 The singer is singing. She's wearing a .... dress.

4 The businesswoman is walking to work. She's wearing a .... ring on her finger.

5 The painter is painting a picture. He's got a big paint .... on his shirt!

6 The journalist is holding an .... because it's raining.

6 Ask and answer.

silver belt

a bag with a black stripe

a uniform

gloves

a big pocket

black tights

striped shorts

Who's got a silver belt?

The singer.

Remember!

who + is = who's
who + has = who's

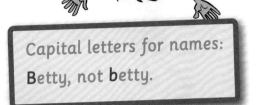

Remember!

Capital letters for names:
Betty, not betty.

Step 2 – Practise

1 Listen and write the names. 2

1   Betty   2 ....   3 ....   4 ....

2 Listen and draw lines. 3

1   Harry
2   David
3   Emma
4   Emma's mum
5   Robert's dad
6   Peter and Helen

Remember!
Draw clear lines.

3 Ask and answer.

What's Harry doing?

He's playing football.

Step 3 – Pass!

1 Listen and draw lines. There is one example. 🎧 4

Betty   Richard   Michael   Helen

Robert   Emma   Katy   William

Listening PART 2

Step 1 – Prepare

1 Write the school subjects. Listen and check. 5

1 science   **2** ....   **3** ....   **4** ....

5 ....   **6** ....   **7** ....   **8** ....

2 Cover the words in exercise 2. Ask and spell.

How do you spell 'art'?

a-r-t

3 Listen and write the words. 6

| drums | pyramids | glue | flags | scissors | dictionary | ~~castle~~ |

1 There's a ...... castle ...... on my history book. It's got two ....

2 I'm learning the .... in my music lesson.

3 We learnt about the .... of Egypt in our history lesson.

4 Can I use your ...., please?

5 I need some .... and .... for my art lesson.

4 Circle the correct words.

1 It's **midday** / **midnight**.

2 It's **half past ten** / **ten to six**.

3 It's **ten minutes past eleven** / **five to two**.

4 It's quarter **past** / **to** five.

5 It's **midday** / **midnight**.

6 It's **quarter past nine** / **quarter to three**.

5 Look and write the words.

This is the Year 6 class. It's Monday. The teacher
is ❶ ...*standing*... in front of the board.
The subject is ❷ ....
The ❸ .... are sitting at their desks.
They're writing an ❹ ....
Their books aren't on the desks, they're in their
❺ .... There's a clock above the
❻ .... , and a ❼ ....
in the corner of the classroom.

6 Draw lines to match the questions and answers.

1 What day is it?   It's above the shelf.

2 What subject is it?   It's ten o'clock.

3 What are they writing?   It's Monday.

4 What's the time?   Maths.

5 Where are the students' books?   An exam.

6 Where is the clock?   In their rucksacks.

Remember!

Monday, not monday

9

Step 2 – Practise

1 **Look and write the school subjects.**

9 a.m.	9.45 a.m.	10.30 a.m.	11.15 a.m.	12 p.m.	1.20 p.m.	2.10 p.m.
shiroyt	thams	grhapyeog	cnicese	LUNCH	rat	sumic
a history	**b**	**c**	**d**		**e**	**f**

1 What time does the history class start? ..... nine o'clock. .....

2 What time does the art class finish? ....

3 What's the third subject of the day? ....

4 What subject is after lunch? ....

5 What is the last subject of the day? ....

6 What starts at midday? ....

7 What subject starts at quarter past eleven? ....

2 **Ask and answer.**

What time does the maths class start?

Quarter to ten.

3 **Listen and circle the words.** 🎧 7

Club: art / music

1 When: Friday / Monday

2 Where: in the art classroom / in the sports centre

3 Time: after school / at lunch time

4 How long is the lesson? one hour / half an hour

5 How many students: 14 / 40

Step 3 – Pass!

1 **Listen and write. There is one example.** 8

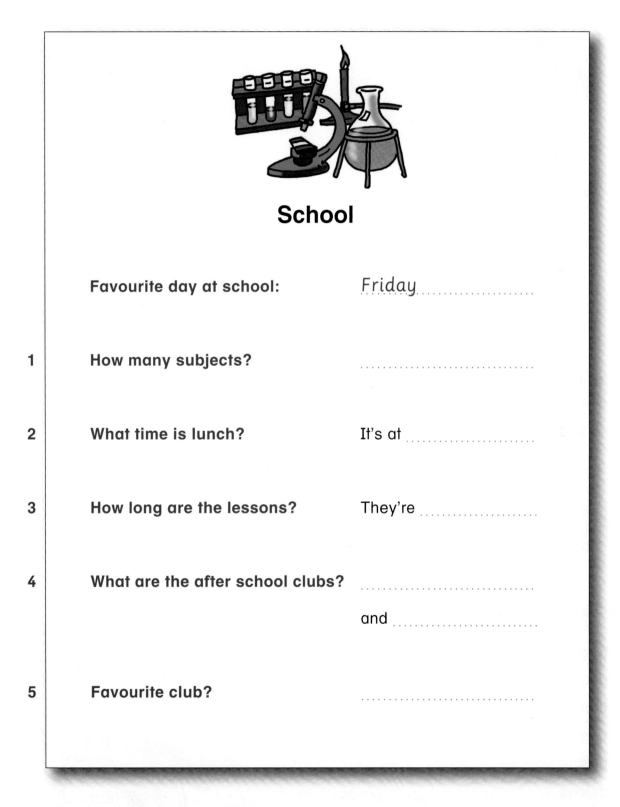

School

Favourite day at school:	*Friday*
1 **How many subjects?**	....
2 **What time is lunch?**	It's at ....
3 **How long are the lessons?**	They're ....
4 **What are the after school clubs?**	....
	and ....
5 **Favourite club?**	....

Step 1 – Prepare

a

b

c

d

1 Match the pictures and the seasons.

| c | summer | | autumn | | spring | | winter |

2 Listen and match the pictures from exercise 1 to the names. 9

| c | Sarah | | Michael | | Emma | | Harry |

3 Find these words in the pictures in exercise 1. Look and write.

1 folg .... *golf* ....
2 nett ....
3 thole ....
4 tusiseca ....
5 ksis ....
6 delegs ....
7 namwons ....
8 lalbwons ....

Use **going to** for future plans!

Remember!

4 Write the words. Do the crossword.

t
o
r
c
h

Across

TEAM A	TEAM B
5	2

1 I play volleyball in the school ....

3 What are you going to do tomorrow? Look in your ....

4 Look! We're running a .... and I'm in front!

5 My football team is going to .... the match!

Down

1 You use this to see in the dark. Take it with you when you go camping!

2 Jill's bought a new ....

5 Look at the pictures again. Circle the correct word.

1 They're sleeping in a **hotel /** (**tent**)

2 The **magazine / diary** is open.

3 They're playing **volleyball / golf**.

4 Volleyball Team **A / B** is winning.

5 The **score / torch** is 5 – 2.

Step 2 – Practise

Listen to the whole dialogue, then answer!

1 Listen and number the pictures in the correct order. 🎧 10

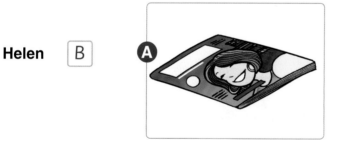

2 Listen. Write A or B in the box. 🎧 11

Helen [B]

Michael [ ]

Katy [ ]

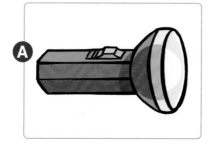

Step 3 – Pass!

1 People are talking about their favourite holidays. 🎧 12
Listen and write a letter in each box. There is one example.

David [H]

Richard [ ]

Betty [ ]

Sarah [ ]

Michael [ ]

Mrs Brown [ ]

A

B

C

D

E

F

G

H

Listening PART 4

Step 1 – Prepare

1 Draw lines to match the words and the pictures.

1 window

glass

2 stamp

paper

3 scarf

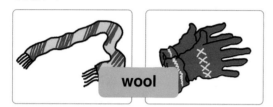
wool

4 ring

gold or silver

5 table

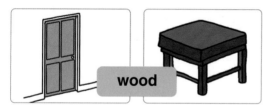
wood

6 comb

plastic

7 key

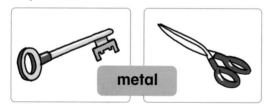
metal

8 box

card

2 Write the words. Listen and check. 13

1 Combs are made of ...plastic... .

2 Stamps are made of ....

3 A key is made of ....

4 A table is made of ....

5 Boxes are made of ....

6 A scarf is made of ....

7 A ring is made of ....

8 Windows are made of ....

3 Find and circle seven objects in the wordsearch.

1

e	n	v	e	l	o	p	e
c	p	k	o	s	o	h	b
s	h	e	l	f	k	o	r
k	o	y	u	r	e	n	u
e	f	r	i	d	g	e	s
c	o	o	k	e	r	b	h

7

2

6

3 　**4** 　**5**

4 Write the objects in exercise 3 and the materials.

	Object	Material
1	brush	plastic / wood
2		
3		
4		
5		
6		
7		

5 Think of the materials. Circle the odd one out. 🎧 14
Listen and check.

1	stamp	magazine	(hat)
2	newspaper	window	glass
3	comb	uniform	toy
4	cooker	desk	fridge
5	box	birthday card	CD
6	T-shirt	scarf	sweater

Listening PART 4

Step 2 – Practise

1 **Listen and tick ✔ the box.** 🎧 15

Listen to the whole dialogue, then answer!

A  B 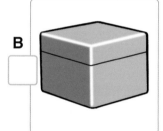 C

2 **Listen again and tick ✔ the box.** 🎧 16

1 John was **on a swing** ☐ **in the garden** ✔ when he found the bag.

2 The bag was made of **paper** ☐ **plastic** ☐ .

3 The box was made of **wood** ☐ **wool** ☐ .

4 The key in the box was made of **gold** ☐ **metal** ☐ .

5 There was a **letter** ☐ **card** ☐ in the envelope.

6 The **stamp** ☐ **comb** ☐ was very old.

Step 3 – Pass!

1 **Listen and tick ✔ the box. There is one example.** 🎧 17

What did Jane lose at the swimming pool?

A  ☐

B  ☐

C 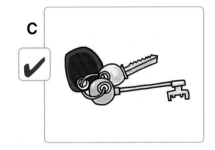 ✔

1 Which bowl did William buy for his mother?

A ☐

B ☐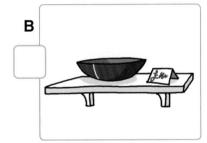

C ☐

2 Where is the telephone in Emma's house?

A ☐

B ☐

C ☐

3 Where did Harry go last summer?

A ☐

B ☐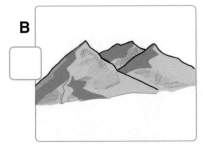

C ☐

Step 1 – Prepare

1 Circle the correct word.

1 (left) / right   2 friendly / unfriendly   3 warm / cold

4 low / high   5 heavy / light

2 Write the opposites of the underlined words and do the crossword.

1 This blanket is so nice and <u>soft</u> – let's sit on it, because the ground is too .... hard ....

2 Your room is very ....! I like my room to be <u>tidy</u>.

3 This bag is very .... It isn't <u>light</u>.

4 Is your dog <u>friendly</u> or ....?

5 Don't turn <u>left</u>. Turn ....

6 That <u>high</u> tree is dangerous. Please climb a .... tree.

7 It isn't <u>cold</u> today. It's ....

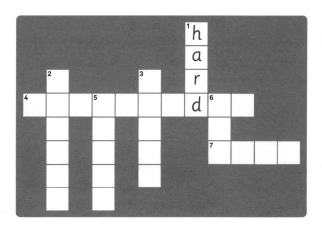

3 Ask and answer. Listen and check. 🎧 18

What's the opposite of tidy?

Untidy.

How do you spell it?

u-n-t-i-d-y

4 **Look and write the words.**

bored	different	enough
excited	far	~~horrible~~	lovely
near	same	too little

1 Queen Jane is ...horrible... but Queen Anne is ....

2 These books are the .... but these books are ....

3 There's .... water in this glass but there's .... water in this glass.

4 Harry is .... but Peter is ....

5 This building is .... but that one is ....

5 **Ask and answer.**

What's the opposite of horrible?

Lovely!

6 **Write the words.**

1 I like your coat. It's ...lovely... .

2 You've got fair hair, and your brother's got brown hair. You don't look the ....

3 We can't swim to the island. It's too ....

4 I'm .... Let's do something interesting.

5 We can't make a cake. We haven't got .... flour. There's too little.

6 It's Sarah's birthday tomorrow. She's very ....

Step 2 – Practise

1 Circle the correct words.

1 The children are having a (lovely) / **horrible** time in the park.

2 The dog can't get the ball in the lake – it's too **near / far**.

3 The kite is flying **high / low**.

4 The kite is **light / heavy**.

5 The children are having a picnic on a **soft / hard** blanket.

6 The man in the café looks **untidy / unfriendly**, because the boy is playing a drum.

Remember! Listen carefully. Don't colour everything!

2 Listen and colour the picture in exercise 1. 19

3 Look at the picture in exercise 1. Listen and write. 20

Step 3 – Pass!

1 Listen and colour and write and draw. There is one example. 21

Remember! Some jobs have m
and female forms: actor / actre
policeman / policewoman.

Step 1 – Prepare

1 Write the words and find Jim's job.

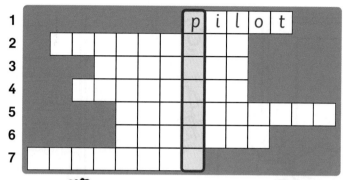

						p	i	l	o	t	
2											
3											
4											
5											
6											
7											

He's a ....

2 Look and write.

1 You go here when you are hungry. ...... café ......
2 You travel in this if you don't have a car. ....
3 You visit this place if you want to learn about history. ....
4 You go here if you want to buy medicine. ....
5 You visit this person if you feel ill. ....
6 You can read stories by journalists in these. ....

3 Read and write the best jobs for these children.

1 I want to make people laugh. I want to work in a circus. ...... clown ......
2 I'm going to visit space in a rocket. ....
3 I want to work in the theatre or on television. ....
4 I love flying. I'm going to learn to fly a plane. ....
5 I'm good at cooking. I'm going to work in a restaurant. ....
6 I'll work in an office and write stories for a newspaper. ....

4 Complete the questions with *How, What* or *Where*.

1 .....What..... do you do?
2 .... do you work?
3 .... do you get to work?
4 .... long does it take?
5 .... far is it?
6 .... is the hospital like?

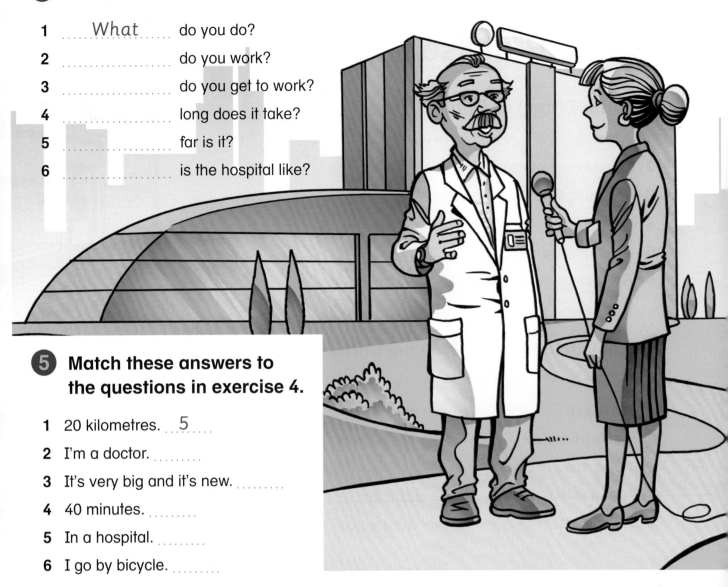

5 Match these answers to the questions in exercise 4.

1 20 kilometres. ..5..
2 I'm a doctor. ....
3 It's very big and it's new. ....
4 40 minutes. ....
5 In a hospital. ....
6 I go by bicycle. ....

6 Work with a partner. Partner A, choose a job. Partner B, ask questions.

What do you do?

I'm a waiter.

Where do you work?

I work in a ...

25

Reading & Writing PART 1

Step 2 – Practise

1 Write **T** (true) or **F** (false).

1 A restaurant is a place where you can eat and sleep. ....F....
2 You can buy medicine at a post office. ....
3 You go to the station if you want to catch a train. ....
4 A university is a place where you can study. ....
5 A meeting is a meal with meat in it. ....
6 Astronauts are people who work in the circus. ....

2 Look at the letters. Write the words. Then draw lines.

1 An **catro** ..._actor_... is a man ⌐ who takes photos for a newspaper.
2 A **nigsre** .... is a person │ who helps you if you have toothache.
3 A **rifenamow** .... is a woman │ who is very good at football.
4 A **regotporhahp** .... is a person └ who works in a theatre.
5 A **nedstit** .... is a person who is good at singing.
6 A **tobolafler** .... is a person who works in a fire station.

3 Circle and write.

1 an artist / (a policeman)   This man wears a uniform. _a policeman_
2 a tennis player / a painter   This person plays a sport. ....
3 an office / a chemist   Businessmen and women work in this place. ....
4 an airport / a factory   They make cars here. ....
5 waiters / secretaries   These people work in an office. ....
6 engineers / painters   These people are artists. ....

> Remember! Copy the words carefully!

26

Step 3 – Pass!

1 **Look and read. Choose the correct words and write them on the lines. There is one example.**

a pilot

traffic

hotel

an ambulance

a café

a journalist

a newspaper

Example

This person flies a plane. ......*a pilot*......

Questions

1 You go to the hospital in this if you are hurt. ....

2 This person writes in a newspaper about things that have happened. ....

3 Firemen and firewomen work in this place. ....

4 This woman works in a theatre or on television. ....

5 Policemen and policewomen work in this place. ....

6 This person works in a kitchen and makes meals. ....

7 These people work in hospitals with doctors. ....

8 This is another word for 'bike'. ....

9 You can have a drink and a snack here with your friends. ....

10 This is the name for cars, buses, lorries and motorbikes on the street. ....

nurses

an actress

a fire station

a cook

a police station

a bicycle

a taxi

Step 1 – Prepare

1 **Look and write the directions.**

on the left / on the right /
on Queen Street but
at the end / at the corner

1 on the right

2 s _ _ _ _ g _ t _ n

3 at _ h _ c _ _ n _ r

4 t _ _ n l _ _ t

5 a _ th _ e _ _

6 _ ur _ ri _ _ t

7 _ n t _ _ l _ _ t

2 **Look and read. Write the words.**

1 It's at the corner next to the college.
   the restaurant

2 It's on Queen Street, on the left, next to the supermarket. ....

3 The bus has just driven past it.
   ....

4 It's between the hotel and the bridge.
   ....

5 Look at the market. This place is on the left. ....

6 It's on the corner of Queen Street, next to the chemist. ....

supermarket
chemist
post office
Queen Street
bookshop
park
police station
King Street
market
factory
college
hotel
restaurant
fire station

3 **Choose a place in the picture. Then ask and answer.**

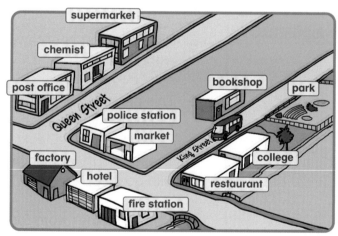

It's next to the college.

The restaurant?

No.

The park?

Yes.

4 Look and circle *yes* or *no*.

1 The college is on Queen Street. **yes** / no

2 The bus is driving past the theatre. **yes** / **no**

3 The hotel is between the factory and the restaurant. **yes** / **no**

4 The chemist is at the corner. **yes** / **no**

5 A car is driving over the bridge. **yes** / **no**

6 The fire station is near the river. **yes** / **no**

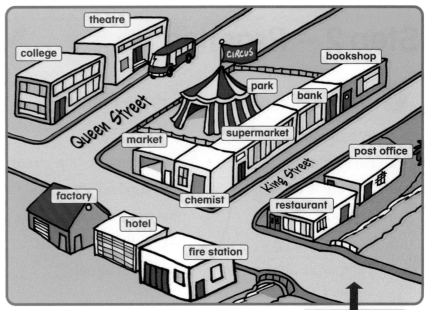

5 Look, read and write. Where are you?

1 Go over the bridge. Turn right and go straight on. It's at the end of the street on the left.
   the bookshop

2 Go over the bridge. Go straight on. It's on the right next to the chemist. ....

3 Go over the bridge and go straight on. Go past the factory and turn right, it's on the corner on the left. ....

4 Go over the bridge. Go past the fire station. It's on the left next to the hotel.
   ....

5 Go over the bridge. Don't turn right. Go straight on. Go past the market and turn right. It's in the park on the right. ....

6 Go over the bridge. Turn right into King Street. It's on the right opposite the supermarket.
   ....

6 Ask and answer.

Excuse me. How do you get to the bookshop?

Go over the bridge, turn right and go straight on. It's at the end of the street on the left.

29

Step 2 – Practise

1 **Look at the picture and draw lines.**

1   He's flying — to the post office.
2   He's pointing — at the corner of the street.
3   The car is driving — between two shops.
4   The post office is — past the post office.
5   There's a lamp — next to the post office.
6   The purple shop is — above the street.

2 **Circle the correct words.**

1   There is someone **between** / **opposite** the man and the girl on the bike.
2   The chemist is **behind / next to** the bookshop.
3   The clothes shop is next to the bookshop on the **left / right**.
4   A man is walking **through / past** the bookshop.
5   A man is walking **into / out of** the bookshop.
6   The bookshop is **between / inside** the clothes shop and the chemist.

3 **Look and read. Write *yes* or *no*.**

> Remember! Only write 'yes' if the whole sentence is true.

1   A woman is going into the chemist with her son. ..yes..
2   The woman's son is carrying a bag. ....
3   A woman is walking past the bookshop. ....
4   The man who is coming out of the bookshop is carrying a bag. ....
5   A girl is riding her bike past the clothes shop. ....
6   The girl has got a rucksack. ....

Step 3 – Pass!

1 **Look and read. Write *yes* or *no*.**

Examples

There are five cars.	..yes..
The museum is next to the chemist.	..no..

Questions

1 A girl is riding her bicycle over the bridge. ....

2 Two women are walking across the street. ....

3 The chemist is on the left of the street. ....

4 A man is walking past the police station. ....

5 A red car is turning left. ....

6 The post office is on the corner. ....

7 The yellow bus has just stopped outside the cinema. ....

Step 1 – Prepare

1 Write the words and find out what Katy is making.

1 v e g e t a b l e s

I'm making ....

2 Look at the pictures in exercise 1. Write *H* next to the healthy foods.

3 Talk to a friend. What food should / shouldn't you eat every day?

You should eat vegetables every day.

You shouldn't eat pizza every day.

4 Circle and write the words. Which is the odd word?

1 ...... *plate* ......
2 ....
3 ....
4 ....
5 ....
6 ....
7 ....

ppl**ate**ispoonnsaltspepperysnowmanforkcknifets

5 Write the words from exercise 4.

1 **Jane:** Have you ever eaten with chopsticks?

 Paul: Yes, I have, but I prefer using a ..... *knife* ..... and ....

2 **Peter:** This pasta doesn't taste very good.

 Daisy: Would you like some .... and .... on it?

 Peter: Yes, please.

3 **John:** Is the table ready for dinner?

 Mum: I need one more .... for the bread and a .... for the soup.

6 Look and write. Then ask a friend.

1 Have you ever ..... *eaten* ..... **(eat)** octopus?
2 Have you ever .... **(try)** carrot cake?
3 Have you ever .... **(use)** chopsticks?
4 Has your mum ever .... **(make)** jam?
5 Have you ever .... **(taste)** vegetable soup?

Have you ever eaten octopus?

No, I haven't.

Step 2 – Practise

1 **Read and draw lines.**

1 What's your meal like?
2 Have you ever eaten here before?
3 What are you going to eat?
4 What were you doing?
5 Where shall we eat?
6 How do you get to the café?

We could go to the café.
I was waiting for you.
It's lovely.
Go straight on. It's on the left.
I'm going to eat pizza.
Yes, we have.

2 **Circle the correct words.**

Ben: What's your favourite food?

Vicky: I **like** / liking pizza.

Ben: Have you ever **been / eat** to a pizza restaurant?

Vicky: Yes, I **have / do**.

Ben: Where **did / have** you go?

Vicky: **I've been / I went** to a pizza restaurant in town.

Ben: What **did you eat / were you eating**?

Vicky: **I ate / I was eating** cheese and tomato pizza and salad.

Ben: That sounds good!

3 **Look and write.**

took	~~make~~	smells	mixed	flour	long	like

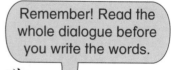

Remember! Read the whole dialogue before you write the words.

Katy: Did you _____make_____ that cake?

Jill: Yes, I did.

Katy: How did you make it?

Jill: I _____ the butter and sugar in a bowl. Then I added the eggs and _____.

Katy: How _____ did it take?

Jill: It _____ one hour.

Katy: It _____ good. What does it taste _____?

Jill: Mmm! It tastes good!

Step 3 – Pass!

1 **William is talking to his mum. What does his mum say?**
Read the conversation and choose the best answer. Write a letter
(A-G) for each answer. You do not need to use all the letters.

Example

William: What are we going to do at the weekend?

Mum: D ....

Questions

1 **William:** What's the restaurant like?

Mum: ....

2 **William:** Where is it?

Mum: ....

3 **William:** Have we eaten there before?

Mum: ....

4 **William:** What did we eat?

Mum: ....

A Yes, we have.

B Yes, I'd like that.

C It's at the corner of the street near the cinema.

D We're going to eat in a restaurant.

E It's very good.

F We ate meat and vegetables.

G It likes good food.

Step 1 – Prepare

1 Write the words and then number the months in order.

☐ J _ _ _	☐ D _ _ _ _ _ _ _	☐ J _ _ _
1 January	☐ M _ _	☐ A _ _ _ _
☐ A _ _ _ _ _	☐ M _ _ _ _	☐ S _ _ _ _ _ _ _ _
☐ F _ _ _ _ _ _	☐ O _ _ _ _ _ _	☐ N _ _ _ _ _ _ _

2 Look and write the words.

1 There are 30 days in April, June, September and November .

2 Christmas Day is on the .... December.

3 The day after the 31st January is the .... February.

4 The last day of the year is the .... December.

5 ...., July and August are in summer in Europe.

6 .... is the shortest month.

Remember! Write 20th June but say the twentieth of June.

3 Ask and answer.

What date is it today?

It's the fifth of April.

When's your birthday?

It's on the twentieth of June.

4 Look and write *in, on* or *at*.

1 His birthday is .....in..... July.

2 My birthday is .... 15th October.

3 My party is on Saturday .... six o'clock.

4 I like going to the beach .... the summer.

5 We're going to go on holiday .... August.

6 We got home .... midday.

5 Look and draw lines to match the sentence halves.

1 We can go to the cinema   if it's sunny.

2 We might go to the beach   so I went by bus.

3 I didn't want to walk   so I'll have a party.

4 I started playing football   when I was six.

5 I was walking home   if it rains.

6 My birthday is in March   when I saw Mary.

6 Ask and answer.

37

Reading & Writing PART 4

Step 2 – Practise

1 **Circle the correct words.**

1 I forgot my books **so** / **if** I was late.
2 I brush my teeth **until** / **before** I go to bed.
3 I was walking home **when** / **after** I saw her.
4 We can play tennis **so** / **if** it doesn't rain.
5 He was still tired **after** / **when** eight hours in bed.
6 I was late **if** / **so** I ran to school.

2 **Look and write. Then number the sentences in order.**

midnight
found
walking
~~April~~
coats
until

[ ] We walked in the storm for an hour before we .... a cave.

[ ] We waited in the cave .... it was dark.

[ ] We stopped and put on our ....

[1] One afternoon in ..... April ..... we decided to go for a walk.

[ ] We got home at ....

[ ] We were .... in the hills when it started to rain.

Remember! Think about which type of word could go in each gap!

3 **Write the words in order to find the title.**

the storm A hills in ....

Step 3 – Pass!

1 **Read the story. Choose a word from the box.**
Write the correct word next to numbers 1-5.
There is one example.

When my friend Helen went on holiday she couldn't take her dog Buster,
.........*so*......... he stayed at our house.

One day, I took Buster for a walk. When we left the house it was dry and
sunny, but later it was windy and the **1**.................... was black. We were
walking up the hill into the woods when it started to rain. 'There's going to be
a **2**...................,' I thought.

Buster wasn't very happy. He didn't like storms. We were walking
3.................... the woods when suddenly Buster ran away. I ran after
him but I couldn't catch him.

I looked for Buster for an hour and I called his name, but I couldn't find him.
I **4**.................... to go home. On my way home I was walking past
Helen's house when I saw Buster. He was waiting in front of the door. He was
cold and wet and he was still afraid. 'There's **5**.................... there,
Buster,' I said. 'Come home with me. '

I took Buster home and gave him a delicious meal. He lay down in front of the
fire and he slept for three hours.

Example
no-one   ~~so~~   sky   decided   air   month
storm   through   waiting   foggy

6 Now choose the best name for this story. Tick ✔ one box.

A walk in the woods ☐

A bad day for Buster ☐

Buster's holiday ☐

39

Step 1 – Prepare

1 Look and draw lines to match the opposite adjectives.

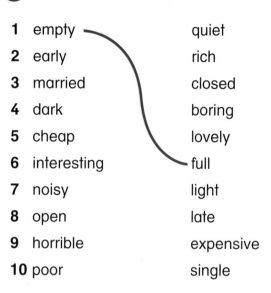

1	empty	quiet
2	early	rich
3	married	closed
4	dark	boring
5	cheap	lovely
6	interesting	full
7	noisy	light
8	open	late
9	horrible	expensive
10	poor	single

2 Look and write adjectives from exercise 1.

1 On Sundays lots of shops aren't ......*open*...... . They're ...*closed*... .

2 I don't like history. It's .... It isn't ....

3 The bus wasn't .... It was .... of people.

4 On weekdays I get up .... for school. At the weekend I stay in bed and I get up ....

5 In the summer the days are long. It's .... at 5.00 a.m. and it's .... at 10.00 p.m.

6 At school we are very .... in the playground, but in the library, we have to be ....

3 Talk to a friend. Disagree.

I think museums are interesting.

Do you? I think they're boring!

4 Look and write. Then order the story A to D.

every   rich   poor   secret   ~~gold~~   unhappy

☐ Then, one day the woman met the king at the secret place and he said 'I've got something for you.' He gave her a small box. Inside the box there was a **1** ....gold.... ring. The king and the woman were married. They lived together in the old castle on the hill.

☐ The king wrote a letter and put it in an envelope with a map. He sent the letter to the young woman's address. The woman opened the envelope and read the letter. It said 'Look at the map. Meet me at the **2** .... place.'

☐ The young woman went to the secret place and the king was waiting for her. They walked and they talked and soon they were good friends. They met **3** .... day for a month.

A Many years ago, a king lived in an old castle on a hill. He had lots of money and he was very **4** ...., but he was **5** .... One day he was riding his horse in the woods when he saw a beautiful woman. She was very **6** .... and she lived in small house. He followed her to back to her little house and wrote down the address.

5 Look and write *so* or *because*.

1 The man was rich ...because.. he was the king.
2 The young woman was poor .... she didn't live in a big house.
3 The king followed her .... he wanted her address.
4 He needed her address .... he wanted to send her a letter.
5 He sent her a map .... that she could find the secret place.
6 He gave her a ring .... he loved her.

6 Look and write *Who, Where, Why, How, What*. Then ask and answer.

1 ...Who.... was rich but unhappy?
2 .... was the king doing when he saw the young woman?
3 .... did the poor woman live?
4 .... did the king follow her?
5 .... did he send her?
6 .... often did they meet at the secret place?

Who was rich but unhappy?

The king.

41

Reading & Writing PART 5

Step 2 – Practise

1 **Read and draw lines to make part of a story.**

1 Robert followed Harry — and saw Grandfather.
2 Harry was carrying — up the stairs.
3 Suddenly they heard — sleeping in a chair!
4 It sounded like — a torch.
5 They opened the door — a lion.
6 He was — a strange noise.

2 **Read and tick ✔ the best words to complete the sentences.**

1 Harry had a torch
  ✔ because it was dark.
  ☐ so it was dark.

2 They walked slowly
  ☐ outside.
  ☐ upstairs.

3 They were afraid because
  ☐ he opened the door.
  ☐ they heard a strange noise.

4 It sounded
  ☐ like an animal.
  ☐ like Grandfather.

5 When they got to the top of the stairs they
  ☐ opened the door.
  ☐ closed the door.

6 Grandfather
  ☐ were in bed.
  ☐ was sleeping.

3 **Look and write the words.**

| pushed | ~~dark~~ | sleeping | laughed | following | sounded |

It was **1** _dark_ . Robert had a torch. I was
2 .... Robert up the stairs when we heard
a noise. It **3** .... like a lion. We were afraid.
We came to a door. Robert **4** .... the door
open slowly. Then he **5** .... It wasn't a lion.
It was his grandfather. He was **6** .... in a chair.

Step 3 – Pass!

1 **Look at the picture and read the story. Write some words to complete the sentences about the story. You can use 1, 2, 3 or 4 words.**

The secret door

My name's Tom. Last week I visited an old castle with my class. We left early in the morning and we went by bus with our history teacher. It took an hour to get to the castle and we sang songs on the bus. It was very noisy!

We visited the castle gardens. They were very interesting. Then we had lunch in the café. Then we went inside the castle and visited all the old rooms. They were full of old paintings. It was boring.

We were looking at the paintings when my friend Harry saw a secret door. Harry and I waited until the room was empty and then we opened the door and went inside. The door closed behind us and we couldn't open it. It was very dark and we were afraid. We could see a small light far away. 'Follow the light,' I said, so Harry and I walked and walked.

At last we came to an open door and we walked outside. The bus was in front of us. We ran to the bus. We were late so everyone was waiting for us. 'Are you OK?' asked our teacher. 'We're fine, thanks,' we said. We didn't tell anyone about our secret.

Example
Tom and his class went by bus to visit an .... *old castle* ....

Questions
1 It was noisy on the bus because ....
2 Before lunch they ....
3 Harry saw the secret door when .... at the paintings.
4 Tom and Harry opened the door and went ....
5 They were afraid because ....
6 Everyone was waiting for them because ....
7 They told .... about their secret.

43

Step 1 – Prepare

1 **Look and write *will* or *won't*.**

In the future …

1 There ......won't...... be any cars.

2 Offices .... be made of glass.

3 People .... go to work by bus.

4 There .... be trees.

5 There .... be robots.

6 More people .... be astronauts.

2 **Talk to a friend. What do you think?**

There won't be any cars.

People will fly to work.

3 **Write P (*in the past*) or T (*today*) or F (*in the future*).**

1 There are lots of cars. ....T....

2 There won't be any water. ....

3 People didn't have computers. ....

4 There weren't any buses. ....

5 We might live on a different planet. ....

6 Every house has got a television. ....

4 **Look and write.**

work	be	buy	~~stay~~	live	fly

1 Will you ..... stay ..... at school until you are 18? ....
2 Will you .... in an office? ....
3 Will you .... to other countries? ....
4 Will you .... rich? ....
5 Will you .... a car? ....
6 Will you .... on the Moon? ....

5 **Read the questions in exercise 4. Put a tick ✔, a cross ✘ or a question mark ? Then ask and answer.**

✔ Yes, I will.
✘ No, I won't.
? I may / might.

Will you stay at school until you're 18?

Yes, I will.

6 **Write sentences about you.**

1 I will stay at school until I'm 18.
2 ....
3 ....
4 ....
5 ....
6 ....

Remember! We use *may* or *might* if we aren't sure about something.

45

Step 2 – Practise

1 Look and draw lines.

I'll be a businesswoman.

1	determiner	job
2	pronoun	a lot
3	verb	in
4	preposition	expensive
5	adjective	fly
6	noun	her

2 Look and write the words from exercise 1.

Remember! Think about which type of word could go in each gap.

1 She'll ...... *fly* ...... around the world. **(verb)**

2 She'll stay .... expensive hotels. **(preposition)**

3 She'll wear .... clothes. **(adjective)**

4 She'll speak .... of languages. **(determiner)**

5 Her .... will be very important. **(noun)**

6 Her secretary will go with .... **(pronoun)**

3 Circle the correct words.

When I leave school I'll **1 (go)/ going** to university. I **2 will / won't** live at the university. I'll live with my friends in the town near the university. I'll stay there **3 when / until** I'm twenty-one, then I'll look for a **4 job / work**. I **5 can't / might** work in a hospital as a nurse or I might decide to be a teacher. I won't be rich, but I'll be happy **6 because / so** my job will be very interesting.

4 Look and write the words.

When I **1** .... *leave* .... school, I'll fly around the world and **2** .... in different countries. I'll work in schools and I'll teach English. I'll meet lots of interesting people. I'll make new friends and I'll learn to **3** .... their languages. I **4** .... be rich or famous, but I'll have an **5** .... time. I **6** .... write a book when I get home.

won't
excellent
live
speak
~~leave~~
might

Step 3 – Pass!

1 **Read the text. Choose the best words and write them on the lines.**

Life in the future

Example	What will the world be like in the future? .... *Will* .... life be the same?
1	Will we .... drive cars made of metal? Will we still read books
2	made of paper? Or will we all .... in houses on the Moon?
3	I believe that life will be very different in the future. We ....
	have televisions, radios or newspapers. We will watch films, listen to music
4	and read the .... on our computers. There won't be any
5	bookshops, because people won't buy books. .... read books
	on their computers, too.
6	People won't drive their cars .... computers will drive for
7	them. Cars might be slower and quieter .... they are today
8	and they won't be dangerous. People will go .... holiday in
	'space planes'. These will fly half way around the world in two hours.
	I think robots will work in factories and they will work for 24 hours a day. They
9	will be .... and faster than people. Medicines will be better
10	and people won't be ill very often. People might live .... they
	are 100 years old. I think life will be very different.

Example	(Will)	Does	Won't
1	just	still	already
2	live	living	will live
3	wouldn't	can't	won't
4	new	news	story
5	They'll	There	Their
6	until	when	because
7	than	then	that
8	in	at	on
9	cheapest	cheaper	more
10	always	when	until

Reading & Writing PART 7

Step 1 – Prepare

1 Write the words in the correct rooms.

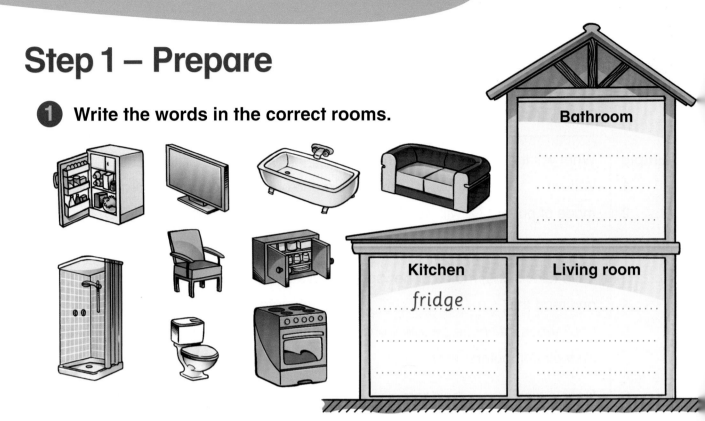

2 Look and write the words.

1 It's a room where there is a bath. <u>bathroom</u>
2 It's something that you cook food on. ....
3 It's made of wood and you put books on it. ....
4 You sit on this when you watch TV. ....
5 You use this to make your hair tidy. ....
6 You turn this on when it's dark. ....

> cooker
> ~~bathroom~~
> light
> shelf
> sofa
> comb

3 Talk to a friend. Play a game.

It's a place in the kitchen where you put food.

A cupboard?

No! It's very cold.

A fridge?

Yes!

4 Look and write the words.

> low ~~soft~~ empty dangerous faster dark

1 They didn't like the sofa because it was too hard. It wasn't ..... soft ..... enough.

2 There wasn't a window in the bathroom, so it was too ....

3 Be careful! The stairs are very old and ....

4 The television was on a .... shelf in the corner.

5 There wasn't any food in the fridge. It was ....

6 It's .... to have a shower than a bath, and it's better for the environment.

5 Look and read. Write *yes* or *no*.

1 The bedroom is very untidy. ..yes..

2 There are books on the shelf. ....

3 It's half past one. ....

4 The door is open. ....

5 The boy is wearing shorts. ....

6 There's a lamp on the desk. ....

6 Ask and answer.

What's your bedroom like?

It's big and it's usually untidy! There's a bed …

Step 2 – Practise

1 Circle the correct words.

My friend Helen came to my house. She's always hungry so we got some flour, butter and chocolate. We ① **ate /** (**made**) chocolate biscuits and cooked them in the ② **oven / fridge**. My bedroom is on the first floor. Helen and I both love listening to ③ **the TV / music** so in the evening, we went ④ **upstairs / downstairs** to my bedroom and listened to some CDs. Helen stayed the night and at midnight we went downstairs. It was very quiet and ⑤ **light / dark**. Helen was afraid so we took a torch. We took the biscuits out of the fridge. Then we went back up to my ⑥ **bathroom / bedroom** and ate them all in bed!

2 Look and write the words.

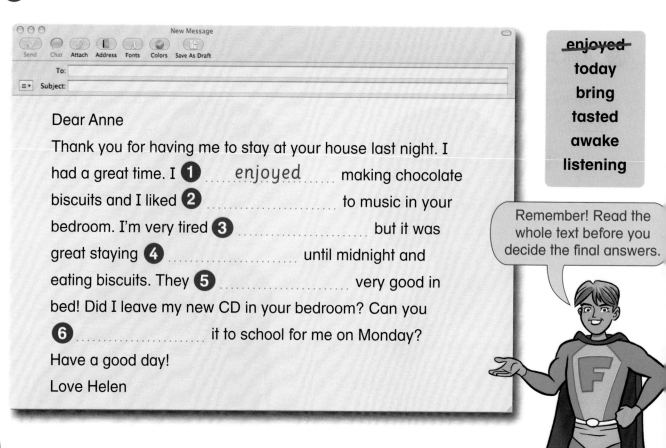

New Message

Send Chat Attach Address Fonts Colors Save As Draft

To:

Subject:

Dear Anne

Thank you for having me to stay at your house last night. I had a great time. I ① *enjoyed* making chocolate biscuits and I liked ② .... to music in your bedroom. I'm very tired ③ .... but it was great staying ④ .... until midnight and eating biscuits. They ⑤ .... very good in bed! Did I leave my new CD in your bedroom? Can you ⑥ .... it to school for me on Monday? Have a good day!

Love Helen

~~enjoyed~~
today
bring
tasted
awake
listening

Remember! Read the whole text before you decide the final answers.

Step 3 – Pass!

1 **Read the letter and write the missing words.**
Write one word on each line.

Dear Mum and Dad

Example   I ......_am_...... camping! The toilets are horrible and

the showers are cold. Last night I lay down in my

1   .... and closed my eyes, but I

2   .... sleep. There were lots of insects in the

3   tent and it was noisy. I woke up very ....

because it was too light.

4   Tomorrow we're going to stay in a ....

5   It isn't cheap, it's .... We're going to have

hot showers, we're going to eat in the restaurant and

we're going to sleep in nice soft beds!

Love from

Richard

Speaking

Step 1 – Prepare

1 Find these things in the pictures. Draw a line to match.

a plane

a letter

a husband

a pocket

a castle

a waiter

2 Ask and answer.

flag   knife
money   ring
stamp   pilot

What's missing in picture 1?

The stamp is missing.

3 Look at exercise 1. Read, circle and write.

1 Is the man posting a postcard? No, he's posting ... *a letter* ... .
   an email   (a letter)   a present

2 Where is the pilot? Is he early? No, he's ....
   excited   bored   late

3 Is the waiter carrying a cake? No, he's carrying a ....
   biscuit   pizza   sweets

4 Are there spots on the flag? No, there are ....
   letters   pictures   stripes

5 Are they married? Yes, they are. She's his ....
   wife   surname   husband

6 Is the watch cheap? No, it's ....
   dangerous   expensive   soft

4 Listen and number the pictures in order. 22

a

b

c 1

d

5 Write the words in order to make questions.

1 Mrs Brown / Why / go / airport / to / the / did / ?
Why did Mrs Brown go to the airport?

2 did / she / her / with / take / What / ?
....

3 travel / How / she / did / ?
....

4 airport / did / she / Who / at / meet / the / ?
....

5 have / dinner / she / Where / did / ?
....

6 read / When / she / the / letter / did / ?
....

6 Ask and answer.

Why did Mrs Brown go to the airport?

Because she had to go to a meeting.

53

Speaking

Step 2 – Practise

1 Look at picture A. Find these and circle.

1 It's an old castle.
2 They're married.
3 She's wearing a gold ring.
4 The taxi door is closed.
5 There's a flag.
6 There are two suitcases.

2 Look at picture B. Put a tick ✔ or a cross ✘.

Draw a clear tick or cross inside the box!

1 ✘ The man standing next to the taxi isn't the woman's husband.

2 ☐ The flag has got a stripe with a spot on it.

3 ☐ The hotel door is open.

4 ☐ The taxi driver is carrying two suitcases.

5 ☐ The man's wife is sitting in the taxi.

6 ☐ There's a castle on the hill.

3 Look at the pictures and make questions. Then match to the answers.

1 Which country / Mr Peters / visit last week?

Which country did Mr Peters visit last week?

2 How / he / travel? ....

3 What colour / his suitcase? ....

4 What / happen / in his hotel room? ....

5 How / he / find / Mrs Wilkins' address? ....

6 Where / he and Mrs Wilkins / meet? ....

a In the hotel restaurant. ....

b It was blue. ....

c There was a letter in the suitcase. ....

d America. ....1....

e By plane. ....

f He saw that he had the wrong suitcase! ....

4 Match the pictures in exercise 3 and the sentences.

1 Oh, no! This isn't my suitcase. Here's an envelope.
I'll find the phone number for this address. ....c....

2 When I get to the hotel, I'm going to have a swim! ....

3 Hello, Mr Peters. Thank you for bringing my suitcase! ....

4 I'm going to America! Here's my suitcase. ....

Speaking

Step 3 – Pass!

Find the differences

Information

	A Jane	B Robert
Where / going to go next summer?	camping	?
How / going to go there?	by train	?
What / going to take?	a rucksack with a tent	?
Who / going to go with?	her class	?
What / going to do there?	go swimming, visit a castle	?

Story

Listening

Part 1 (5 questions)

Listen and draw lines. There is one example. 23

Sarah　David　Michael　Helen

Harry　Emma　Katy　William

Listening

Part 2 (5 questions)

Listen and write. There is one example. 24

AN INTERESTING JOB

	Name:	*Martyn*
1	How old?	
2	Job:	
3	Name of club:	
4	Date of next game:	
5	Time:	

Listening

Part 3 (5 questions)

What did each person buy at the market?

Listen and write a letter in each box. There is one example. 🎧 25

Mrs Swan   C

Mr Swan

Harry

Katy

Richard

Sarah

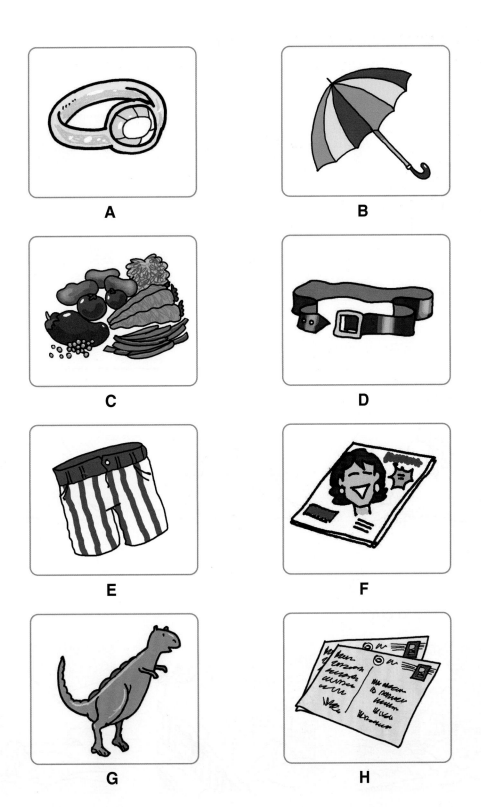

A

B

C

D

E

F

G

H

Listening

Part 4 (5 questions)

Listen and tick ✔ the box. There is one example. 26

What's the weather like?

A

B ☐

C ☐

1 Which snowman has Betty made?

A ☐

B ☐

C ☐

2 Where is she going to go?

A ☐

B ☐

C ☐

3 Who is she going to meet?

A ☐

B ☐

C ☐

4 What is she going to take?

A ☐

B ☐

C ☐

5 What time does she have to come home?

A ☐

B ☐

C ☐

Listening

Part 5 (5 questions)

Listen and colour and write and draw. There is one example. 27

Reading & Writing

Part 1 (10 questions)

**Look and read. Choose the correct words and write them on the lines.
There is one example.**

butterfly

fog

wood

queen

rocket

ring

scissors

Example

You wear this with your trousers
or jeans if they are too big.   ......belt......

Questions

1   It's a beautiful, big, white bird with
    a long neck. It swims on a lake.   ....

2   It takes astronauts up into space.   ....

3   He brings your meals
    in a restaurant.   ....

4   It will help you see in the dark.   ....

5   You can ride on it down a
    mountain in the snow.   ....

6   In this weather, you can't
    see very well.   ....

7   Sweaters, scarves, hats and
    gloves are made of it.   ....

8   She lives in a castle.   ....

9   You use these to cut paper,
    card or plastic.   ....

10 It's a pretty insect.
    It's got four wings.   ....

sledge

glue

swan

camel

torch

waiter

wool

king

Reading & Writing

Part 2 (7 questions)

Look and read. Write *yes* or *no*.

Examples

A swan is taking someone's ice cream. ....no......

A woman is wearing a purple T-shirt and a red hat. ...yes...

PRACTICE TEST

Questions

1 The man, who has had a shower, is carrying a towel.   . . . .

2 A girl has just jumped into the pool.   . . . .

3 The woman at the table is writing postcards.   . . . .

4 A girl's ice cream has just fallen into the pool.   . . . .

5 There are two waiters working at the snack shop.   . . . .

6 There is a boy wearing a striped sweater.   . . . .

7 Two boys have bought ice creams.   . . . .

Reading & Writing

Part 3 (5 questions)

Harry is talking to his friend, Betty. What does Harry say?
Read the conversation and choose the best answer.
Write a letter (A-H) for each answer. You do not need to use all the letters.

Example

Harry: Hi, Betty! What are you going to do today?

Betty: .....C......

Questions

1 **Harry:** Why?

  Betty: ....

2 **Harry:** Are you going to draw a picture on it?

  Betty: ....

3 **Harry:** What kind of picture?

  Betty: ....

4 **Harry:** Here's a nice one. Look, it's a rabbit.

  Betty: ....

5 **Harry:** Of course. Have you got a pair of scissors?

  Betty: ....

A Yes, I like it. Can you cut it out for me?

B She likes animals. Perhaps I'll find something in this animal magazine.

C I'm going to make a card for Sarah.

D No, I'm going to cut out a picture from a magazine.

E Yes, I have. Here you are.

F Because it's her birthday tomorrow.

G No, I don't.

H No, it isn't.

Reading & Writing

Part 4 (6 questions)

Read the story. Choose a word from the box. Write the correct word next to the numbers 1 – 5. There is one example.

Last summer, we went on holiday in the countryside. We didn't want to stay in a

.... *hotel* .... because it was too **1** .... We wanted to

sleep outside, under the **2** ...., in a tent! So we drove to the

mountains and found a quiet place next to the river. We cooked our dinner on a

3 .... that night. We told stories and sang songs. It was fun!

When we got tired, my dad said, 'Time to go to bed! Let's get up early in the

morning and go for a swim in the river!' That night, I had a **4** ....

I was swimming in the river. The water felt cold … Suddenly I woke up. It wasn't a

dream! There was water inside our tent! It was **5** .... very hard,

and the tent was wet. My dad went outside the tent – and walked into the water!

The river was very deep – there was water all around our tent.

We packed our tents up and drove to a hotel. That was the end of our camping

holiday!

Example

hotel   cooker   lovely   dream   expensive

fire   photo   rained   raining   stars

6   Now choose the best name for the story. Tick ✔ one box.

A holiday by the sea ☐

A terrible fire ☐

My camping trip ☐

Reading & Writing

Part 5 (7 questions)

Look at the picture and read the story. Write some words to complete the sentences about the story. You can use 1, 2, 3 or 4 words.

Shell soup

One day a man went to a village. He was carrying a large, empty, metal bowl. He didn't have any food, so he was very hungry. But the people in the village were poor. They didn't have much food, and they were usually very weak and hungry, too. They said, 'We are sorry, but we don't have any food to give you.'

So the man went to the beach and filled the bowl with sea water. He picked up a shell from the beach and put it into the bowl. He put the bowl on a fire to cook.

A farmer from the village looked at the man. 'What are you cooking?' he asked.

The man said, 'It's shell soup.'

The farmer asked, 'Can we have some?'

The man said, 'Yes, you can. But shell soup tastes better with some vegetables. Have you got just one vegetable to put into the soup?'

So the farmer gave the man a carrot and he put it into the bowl to cook with the shell. Then the farmer's wife put a potato into the bowl.

Soon, all the people in the village started to smell the soup and came to see what the man was cooking. They all brought one vegetable to put into the soup: a tomato, an onion, a few beans and some peas.

When the soup was ready, the man said, 'Everybody, bring a spoon to eat the soup. Come and have some lovely soup.'

Everybody enjoyed the soup and said thank you to the man. After that, they were never hungry again. They ate shell soup often and they were healthy and strong.

PRACTICE TEST

Examples

A man went ....*to a village*.... one day.

He was carrying a bowl ...*made of metal*...

Questions

1 The man was hungry because he .... any food.

2 He got some .... the sea and put it into the bowl.

3 On the sand, he found .... and put it into the bowl, too.

4 He started cooking on ....

5 The people in the village could .... something nice cooking.

6 They all put a .... the bowl.

7 Then they all brought .... the soup, and it was very nice.

Reading & Writing

Part 6 (10 questions)

Read the text. Choose the right words and write them on the lines.

Butterflies

Example	There ......*are*...... about 24,000 different kinds of butterflies in
1	the world. Butterflies are .... of different colours. One
2	butterfly is called the Glasswing butterfly .... its wings
3	look like glass! In summer and spring, you .... see lots
4	of butterflies .... the garden. They drink from flowers.
5	They also .... fruit.
6	Butterflies like warm places. Lots of butterflies leave ....
	home countries in the winter and they fly to a warmer country. They
7	don't live .... a long time – eleven months is very old
	for a butterfly.
8	Did you know that butterflies .... see? They can see
9	the colours red, green and yellow. Butterflies .... six
10	legs and feet. They .... taste with their mouths. They
	taste with their feet!

Example	is	(are)	be
1	some	one	lots
2	but	because	how
3	can	do	are
4	on	at	in
5	play	go	like
6	them	they	their
7	in	for	to
8	do	can	did
9	got	not have	have got
10	not	don't	don't like

Reading & Writing

Part 7 (5 questions)

Read the letter and write the missing words. Write one word on each line.

Dear Grandma

Example I'm .... *going* .... to visit a museum with my class next week!

1 Our ...., Miss Smith, wants to show us all the

2 interesting things there. I'm very .... about the trip,

because I like learning about history.

We're going to travel to the museum by bus. We aren't going to eat in

3 the museum restaurant, so we have to take our .... in

4 our rucksacks. Mum is going to make me my .... food:

a chicken sandwich!

5 I'll .... a postcard at the museum and put a stamp on

it. Then I'll write and tell you all about the day.

Love

Sarah

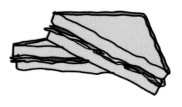

Speaking
Summary of procedures

The usher introduces the child to the examiner. The examiner asks the child what his/her surname is and how he/she is.

1 The examiner shows the child the candidate's copy of the Find the Differences picture. The child is initially shown the examiner's copy as well, then encouraged to look at the candidate's copy only. The examiner then makes a series of statements about the examiner's picture and the child has to respond by making statements showing how the candidate's picture is different, for example *In my picture, a boy is reading a book about London,* and the child answers *In my picture, a boy is reading a book about Paris.*

2 The examiner shows the child the candidate's copy of the Information Exchange. The child is initially shown the examiner's copy as well, then encouraged to look at the candidate's copy only. The examiner then asks the child questions related to the information the child has, for example *Where is Emma going shopping?* and the child answers. The child then asks the examiner questions, for example *What does David want to buy?* and the examiner answers.

3 The examiner tells the child the name of the story and describes the first picture, for example *Making a cake. Katy and Emma are going to make a cake. Katy has got some eggs, flour and butter.* The examiner then asks the child to continue telling the story.

4 The examiner asks questions about the child, for example *What time do you get up in the morning?*

Speaking

PRACTICE TEST

A David's shopping trip

A David		B Emma	
Where / go shopping?	at the supermarket	Where / go shopping?	?
What / he / want to buy?	some soap	What / she / want to buy?	?
Why?	for his mum's birthday	Why?	?
What / smell like?	flowers	What / feel like?	?
he / buy it? Why?	yes, because his mum loves things that smell nice	she / buy it? Why not?	?

B Emma's shopping trip

A David		B Emma	
Where / go shopping?	?	Where / go shopping?	in the market
What / he / want to buy?	?	What / she / want to buy?	a hat
Why?	?	Why?	because the weather was getting colder
What / smell like?	?	What / feel like?	soft and warm
he / buy it? Why?	?	she / buy it? Why not?	no, because it was too expensive

Speaking

Making a cake

Two hours later